# SPIDERS
## ARE AWESOME

by Nancy Furstinger

12 STORY LIBRARY

**www.12StoryLibrary.com**

12-Story Library is an imprint of Bookstaves and Press Room Editions

Produced for 12-Story Library by Red Line Editorial

Photographs ©: PK289/Shutterstock Images, cover, 1; Cornel Constantin/Shutterstock Images, 4; Mirko Graul/Shutterstock Images, 5; Jean and Fred CC 2.0, 6; Sari ONeal/Shutterstock Images, 7, 11; MMCez/Shutterstock Images, 8; IanRedding/Shutterstock Images, 9; asawinimages/Shutterstock Images, 10; Sarah2/Shutterstock Images, 12; kurt_G/Shutterstock Images, 13, 25; Cathy Keifer/Shutterstock Images, 14, 28; zstock/Shutterstock Images, 15; panyawat bootanom/Shutterstock Images, 16; Aleksey Sagitov/Shutterstock Images, 17; cyrrpit/Shutterstock Images, 18; Trevor Holdaway, 19; David Peter Ryan/Shutterstock Images, 20; Arnold John Labrentz/Shutterstock Images, 21, 29; D. Kucharski K. Kucharska/Shutterstock Images, 22; Pavel Krasensky/Shutterstock Images, 23; Heldor/Shutterstock Images, 24; Audrey Snider-Bell/Shutterstock Images, 26, 27

**Library of Congress Cataloging-in-Publication Data**
Names: Furstinger, Nancy, author.
Title: Spiders are awesome / by Nancy Furstinger.
Description: Mankato, MN : 12 Story Library, 2017. | Series: Animals are
   awesome | Includes bibliographical references and index. | Audience:
   Grades 4 to 6.
Identifiers: LCCN 2016046439 (print) | LCCN 2017005248 (ebook) | ISBN
   9781632354419 (hardcover : alk. paper) | ISBN 9781632355096 (pbk. : alk.
   paper) | ISBN 9781621435617 (hosted e-book)
Subjects: LCSH: Spiders--Juvenile literature.
Classification: LCC QL452.2 .F87 2017 (print) | LCC QL452.2 (ebook) | DDC
   595.4/4--dc23
LC record available at https://lccn.loc.gov/2016046439

Printed in China
022017

Access free, up-to-date content on this topic plus a full digital version of this book. Scan the QR code on page 31 or use your school's login at 12StoryLibrary.com.

# Table of Contents

# Spiders Sport Four Pairs of Eyes

Spiders are amazing arachnids. All members of the arachnid family have eight legs that end in claws. Their bodies are divided into two parts. Spiders and their creepy-crawly cousins, such as scorpions, belong to this family. There are approximately 43,200 different species of spiders. They are not insects, because they lack wings and antennae.

Spiders look bizarre. Most sport four pairs of eyes. Some spiders have one huge pair of eyes. For example, net-casting spiders hunt prey at night. They have two huge eyes that help them snag flying and crawling insects in the dark. Then, they stretch their nets to ensnare their victims.

Below a spider's eyes are jaws ending in fangs. All spiders are predators. They seize their prey

A close-up of a jumping spider's eyes

using their mouthparts. Spiders hunt in all types of habitats around the world except for the coldest ones. Some species live in deserts and caves on coastlines. Other spiders live in water.

Spider fossils are often found in amber.

Spiders wear their skeletons on the outside of their bodies. This hard covering is called an exoskeleton. It supports and protects their bodies. Inside, spiders have lungs and hearts. Their hearts pump pale-blue blood.

All spiders spin silk. This strong fiber is made out of strands of protein that spiders produce in their bodies. Then, they push out the silk through special organs called spinnerets. Spiders use the silk to weave webs, including sticky portions to capture prey. They also use silk to move to different locations and to make cocoons for their eggs.

## SPIDER FOSSILS

A close relative of today's spiders lived 305 million years ago. This eight-legged creature existed before dinosaurs. It was preserved in ancient rock in France. Scientists used high-powered X-rays to examine the rock. They saw that the tiny arachnid was less than 0.5 inches (1.3 cm) long. Fossils of other early spiders have been discovered in amber. A piece of amber that dates back 100 million years contains a spider attacking a wasp that was trapped in its web.

## 2
**Pairs of legs spiders hold in the air when they move.**

- Approximately 43,200 species of spiders are found around the world.
- Most spiders have four pairs of eyes.
- Spiders have fangs to seize prey.
- Spiders have pale-blue blood.

# Spiders Dance to Attract Mates

Male peacock spiders work hard to attract females. They use special dance moves. First, they shake a pair of their legs around. Then, they raise a flap over their bellies and wave it like a fan from side to side.

Some male peacock spiders have bright color patterns. Their nicknames are equally colorful. One is called Skeletorus. It has a black body with white stripes. This makes the spider look as if it is wearing a skeleton costume. Another is called Sparklemuffin. It has flashy red stripes that stand out on its blue belly. Most females are different shades of brown.

Peacock spiders are found only in Australia. They are a type of jumping spider. So far, 53 species of peacock spiders have been named. Peacock spiders have tiny bodies. They measure less than 0.25 inches (0.64 cm) long.

The biggest peacock spiders are the size of a pencil eraser.

Black widows are found in the United States, Canada, and Mexico.

Male peacock spiders hope their mating dance will win over the females of their species. However, they run a big risk. If the females become bored by the dance, they gobble up their suitors.

Another female spider that eats her mates is the black widow. The male must find a spot between the female's fangs in order to mate. Afterward, the female may kill the male. Then, she devours him.

The black widow's Australian cousin also eats her mate. The redback male starts off with a mating dance. He bounces up and down on the female's web. During mating he flips toward the female's jaws. Then the female makes a meal of the male.

# 900
**Maximum number of eggs a black widow sac can hold.**

- Australia is the only place where peacock spiders live.
- Peacock spiders are nicknamed for their colors and patterns.
- Male peacock spiders perform dances to attract females.
- Female spiders sometimes eat their mates.

# Mothers Give Spiderlings Piggyback Rides

After mating, female spiders lay eggs. They lay between 2 and 1,000 eggs, depending on the species. Spider mothers protect their eggs by laying them in egg sacs. Each sac is made of spun silk.

Some mother spiders find a safe spot for their egg sacs. They might hide them in a burrow or under bark. Or they might hang them from webs or leaves. Then, the mothers either die or leave.

Other mother spiders stay with their egg sacs. They guard the eggs from predators that might eat them, such as ants and birds. Flies and wasps lay their eggs in the sacs. Later, the baby flies and wasps eat the spider eggs.

Wolf spiders are devoted mothers. They carry their egg sacs everywhere they go. These sacs contain several dozen eggs. The female spider opens the sac using her jaws when

Wolf spiders carry their egg sacs in their spinnerets until they hatch.

# 200

**Number of miles (322 km) spiderlings can drift offshore onto boats using silk strands.**

- Spiders lay their eggs in silk sacs.
- Some spider mothers hide their egg sacs.
- Other spider mothers protect their eggs from predators.
- Wolf spiderlings hitch a ride on their mothers' backs.

## SPIDER RAIN

In Australia in 2015, millions of baby spiders rained down from the sky after they hatched. They needed to find a new spot to live. First, they climbed to the top of a plant or fence post. Then, they jumped and released silk. The strands of silk acted like parachutes. Wind carried the spiders up and away into the air. When they landed in clumps in their new home, the spiders blanketed the ground with silk until it looked like snowfall.

her eggs are ready to hatch. Then, spiderlings emerge and climb up their mother's legs and onto her back. Spiderlings stay with their mothers for several days until they grow big enough to be on their own.

Wolf spiderlings crawl onto their mothers' backs after they hatch.

# Spiders Attack with Poisonous Fangs

A few types of adult spiders can be dangerous to people. A small number of species inject venom that causes discomfort. In rare cases, their bite is deadly. Most poisonous spiders are very timid when it comes to encounters with humans. They usually bite only when surprised or trapped. Few can pierce human skin with their fangs.

The female black widow spider is the most dangerous type of spider in North America. This spider's venom is 15 times more toxic than a rattlesnake's. Females are approximately 1.5 inches (3.8 cm) long. Males are about half this size and are harmless.

Black widows inject poison through their fangs when they bite. They usually do this in self-defense. If a person disturbs them, these spiders will attack. Their bite feels like a pinprick. It can cause pain and cramps. It might make breathing difficult. But their bite is rarely fatal.

A close-up of a tarantula's fangs

Brown recluse spiders live in woodpiles, garbage, and rocks.

The brown recluse spider also has a nasty bite. These tiny spiders are only 0.25 inches (0.64 cm) long. They have a violin-shaped pattern on the front half of their bodies. Brown recluse spiders bite when their hiding spots are disturbed. Their bite can lead to a painful sore that leaves a scar.

People who are bitten by a poisonous spider should seek medical help. Sometimes they will be given an antivenin. This is a medicine that acts against the poison. There is no antivenin for brown recluse spider bites. In the meantime, doctors can use other treatments, such as antihistamines.

## 2,500
**Number of visits Americans make to poison control centers each year after being bitten by a black widow spider.**

- Some spiders are dangerous to humans.
- Female black widow spiders can inject poison.
- The bite of brown recluse spiders can lead to a painful sore.
- Doctors treat some spider bites with an antivenin.

# Spiders Weave Vibrating Funnel Webs

Most spiders seek out insects as prey. They weave different types of webs to catch a meal. Web-building spiders have spinnerets that trail from the tips of their bodies. They use these organs to spin silky thread for their webs.

Funnel-web spiders build a funnel-shaped web. It has a flat surface for catching prey and a tube where the spider lives. The web is made out of dry silk. It lacks any sticky threads. Spiders build funnel webs in grasses and bushes.

When flying or jumping insects fall onto the funnel web's flat surface, the web vibrates to alert the spider. Then, the spider springs into action. It races toward its prey. It grabs the struggling insect. Next, the spider bites the insect and wraps it in silk. It drags its prey back to its tube to eat.

A European funnel web spider guards its nest.

# 3

**Number of feet (0.9 m) in diameter of the largest orb webs.**

- Spiders that build webs have spinnerets to spin silk.
- Funnel webs vibrate when insects land on their flat surface.
- Orb webs capture insects in a sticky spiral.
- Web-building spiders wrap their prey in silk.

## THINK ABOUT IT

The spider in the book *Charlotte's Web* was an orb weaver who spun her famous webs inside a barn. Where else have you seen spiderwebs? What insects have you seen captured in their webs?

Orb-weaver spiders build big, flat webs. Their webs are shaped like large circles and have many smaller circles inside them. Silken spokes extend from the center outward. The spiders weave a sticky spiral into the web to capture their prey.

The orb-weaver spider sits in the middle of its web. Sometimes it hides nearby in leaves or on a branch. A silky trapline vibrates to let the spider know that prey is tangled in the web. Then, the spider quickly wraps the insect in silk and either eats it or stores it for later.

Some people believe spiny orb weavers rebuild their webs often so they are extra strong.

# Spiders Ambush Their Prey

A web is not necessary for some spiders. These species hunt for their meals. They either chase and pounce on their prey or jump out and ambush it.

Wolf spiders were named after the way they hunt. They pursue and jump on their prey the same way wolves do. Their keen eyesight helps them hunt both day and night. Wolf spiders have two huge eyes that face forward and two others that face up. They have four smaller eyes in a row below the four huge eyes.

Wolf spiders hide on the ground in places where their prey, such as crickets and grasshoppers, is found. They live under stones, logs, or dead leaves and in tall grasses. They wait for prey to pass by and then chase it. Long, thin legs help wolf spiders move quickly.

Trapdoor spiders build long tunnels in the ground. They use their mouths to dig. Some species even have rows of spines on their jaws that

A wolf spider with its prey

Trapdoor spiders line their burrows with silk.

help them excavate the ground. They roll the soil into a ball and toss it out of the tunnel using their back legs. Then, they top the entrance with a trapdoor made of soil, moss, and silk. The trapdoor acts like a cork, sealing the spider inside.

Trapdoor spiders hide inside the tunnel and wait for prey, such as beetles, to pass by. If they spot prey, they spring out of the tunnel. They run quickly to ambush insects. Trapdoor spiders are timid. They stay underground inside their tunnels when they are not hunting.

## 20

### Number of years a trapdoor spider can live.

- Some spiders hunt for prey without using webs.
- Wolf spiders use their keen eyesight to spot prey during the day and at night.
- Trapdoor spiders dig tunnels using their mouths.
- Trapdoor spiders hide inside their tunnels until they spot prey.

## INSECT MELTDOWN

How do spiders eat the insects they have captured? First, they spit digestive fluid over their victims. This acts like a meat tenderizer. It turns the insects' muscles and organs into a liquid. Then, spiders chew and suck out the liquid. Finally, they discard the hard parts of the insects, such as their legs and wings.

# Spiders Perform Pest Control and Inspire Scientists

Many people are afraid of spiders. This fear is called arachnophobia. Just the sight of a spider can trigger a rapid heart rate and other symptoms.

Yet spiders offer humans many benefits. Indoors, they help control the insect population. Spiders feast on fleas, flies, mosquitos, and cockroaches. These insects can carry diseases.

Spiders destroy outdoor pests, too. They feed on insects found on farms, such as beetles, aphids, and moths. Without spiders, these insects would destroy crops. Organic farmers welcome spiders to control pests without using chemicals.

Some spiders play an important role

Mosquitoes are a favorite food for spiders.

Spiders make the silk for their webs inside their bodies.

in science. Researchers are testing chemicals found in spider venom. They believe some of the

**614**

**Number of spider species found in croplands in the United States.**

- Spiders eat insects that carry diseases.
- Venom contains chemicals that could help humans.
- Spider silk is tougher than steel.
- Silk could replace heavy protective gear that soldiers wear.

compounds can help control pain. Some researchers are studying a protein found in spider venom. They think it can be used to treat muscular dystrophy.

The silk spiders use to spin their webs is tougher than steel. Researchers believe it could be used to make everything from surgical thread to airplanes. The US Army is experimenting with spider silk to see if it can be used to make protective gear for soldiers. It is very lightweight and could replace the heavy body armor that troops wear while on patrol. This would make the troops serving in hot regions more comfortable.

# Spiders Gobble Bats, Birds, and More

Not all spiders dine solely on insects. Some have unusual diets. The giant golden orb weaver munches on bats. These flying mammals sometimes get entangled in giant webs up to five feet (1.5 m) wide. Then, the spider pounces on its prey.

Other spiders gobble birds. The goliath bird-eating spider prowls the rain forests of South America. It sneaks up on its prey and pounces.

Then, the spider uses its huge fangs to inject poison into the bird, mouse, frog, or snake. However, its favorite meal is earthworms.

The bird-eating spider has other weapons aside from its fangs. It flings tiny barbed hairs at its enemies' skin and eyes. The hairs cause itching and pain. The bird-eating spider also scares off predators by rubbing the bristles on its legs to make a hissing sound.

Curly hair tarantulas are a type of bird-eating spider that live in Costa Rica.

## DEEP-FRIED SPIDERS

In some countries, spiders are considered a tasty snack. They are rich in protein. In Cambodia, people eat fried tarantulas. The spiders are fried in oil until they are crispy. Then, they are seasoned with salt and garlic. Other places in Southeast Asia sell barbecued tarantulas on a stick.

The Australian wolf spider hunts for frogs and cane toads. Millions of toxic cane toads have spread across Australia, where they are considered pests. Wolf spiders either chase down or ambush the toads.

Fish-eating spiders stalk their prey. They hunt for their meals in fresh water, such as ponds and wetlands.

# 15

**Number of feet (4.6 m) from which a goliath bird-eating tarantula's hissing noise can be heard.**

- Some spiders catch bats in gigantic webs.
- Bird-eating spiders make hissing sounds by rubbing the bristles on their legs.
- Wolf spiders ambush toxic cane toads.
- Fish-eating spiders hunt for meals in ponds and wetlands.

They stretch their front legs out on the water's surface and wait for fish. Then, the fish-eating spiders catch their prey and inject it with venom.

Fried spiders are a delicacy in some parts of Cambodia.

# Spiders Have Happy Faces on Their Bellies

Spiders come in different colors and patterns. Crab spiders blend into their environment using camouflage. They can even change colors to match the different flowers where they hide. Predators cannot spot the crab spiders.

The Hawaiian happy-face spider has unique markings on its belly. Its smiley face design confuses birds into thinking that the spiders are not food. The happy-face spider is found on four of the Hawaiian Islands.

Peacock spiders come in colorful patterns. The males have vibrant designs that look similar to the tail feathers of a peacock. They use these hues to attract, rather than repel, females.

The color pattern on a female black widow is meant to ward off enemies. A red hourglass shape appears on her shiny black abdomen. It broadcasts that this spider has a deadly bite.

Orb-web spiders have an unusual way to avoid predators.

A white and magenta crab spider camouflaged on a white rose petal

They decorate their webs with silky spirals and dead leaves. This makes the webs look like bird droppings. The spiders can hide in their webs and hunt prey without being hunted by predators.

The Hawaiian happy-face spider is known as *nananana makaki'i* in Hawaiian. It means "face-patterned spider."

## 1973
**Year Hawaiian happy-face spiders were discovered.**

- Crab spiders can change color to blend into their habitat.
- Hawaiian happy-face spiders have a pattern that confuses predators.
- Male peacock spiders have bright colors to attract females.
- Orb-web spiders decorate their webs to resemble bird droppings.

## THINK ABOUT IT

What experiment could you do to learn more about how crab spiders use camouflage or Hawaiian happy-face spiders use patterns? Think about the questions you want to answer. Then, list the steps you would take to get these answers.

# Diving Bell Spiders Come Up for Air Once a Day

Some spiders enjoy water sports. They can swim and dive. Their watery habitats contain a variety of insects for them to eat.

Fishing spiders are lightweight and have hairy feet. Both of these traits allow them to float on water. These spiders are also skillful swimmers. They use their two middle pairs of legs to row to different locations. If they become frightened, fishing spiders plunge through the water to hide on the bottom.

Below water, fishing spiders use air bubbles trapped on their hairy bodies to breathe. They hunt for fish and tadpoles under the water and insects floating on the surface above them.

Another species of spider prefers to stay submerged in the water. It comes up for air only once per day. Like fishing spiders, diving bell spiders also use air bubbles to breathe underwater. They fill their silk webs with air, using the hairs on their bodies to bring the bubbles below the surface. These bubble webs act like a fish's gills.

Diving bell spiders trap air in the hairs on their legs.

Brainstorm different ways that animals can survive underwater. Pick one characteristic. Then, write a story about how your chosen animal spends a day beneath the water.

Diving bell spiders spend their entire lives underwater. Their bubble webs nestle among water plants. Inside, the spiders catch fish or insects and drag their prey into their webs to eat.

# 60

**Maximum number of minutes a fishing spider can stay underwater.**

- Spiders can plunge into water like a scuba diver.
- Fishing spiders float atop water using their hairy feet.
- Diving bell spiders live underwater thanks to bubble webs that act like gills.

Diving bell spiders live mostly underwater.

# Gigantic Spiders Are the Size of Plates

Jumbo spiders look like they just crawled out of a nightmare. Many spiders are tiny, but a few have incredible leg spans.

Huge, hairy tarantulas are some of the biggest spiders in the world. The goliath bird-eating spider can span up to nearly 12 inches (30 cm) across. It is around the same size as a small pizza. The goliath bird-eating spider also wins the heavyweight champion title. It can weigh up to 2.5 ounces (71 g).

This tarantula possesses an impressive pair of fangs that are one inch (2.5 cm) long. It uses these mouthparts to deliver a fatal bite to birds, rodents, lizards, and crickets.

Two other gigantic tarantulas also snack on mice and crickets. The Brazilian salmon pink bird-eating

The Brazilian salmon pink bird-eating tarantula is one of the largest spiders in the world.

Giant huntsman spiders chase down their prey instead of building webs.

tarantula has a 10-inch (25-cm) leg span. The king baboon tarantula can grow up to nearly eight inches (20 cm) across.

The giant huntsman spider lives up to its name. Its leg span reaches 12 inches (30 cm). This spider is as big as a dinner plate. The giant huntsman earned the nickname "the giant crab spider" for the way it moves. Its twisted leg joints allow the spider to scuttle sideways like a crab. It also can dart across smooth surfaces, such as windows.

# 2001
**Year the giant huntsman spider was discovered in a cave in Laos.**

- Some tarantulas are among the world's biggest, heaviest spiders.
- The goliath bird-eating spider can be almost 12 inches (30 cm) across.
- Enormous spiders eat birds, mice, lizards, and crickets.
- The giant huntsman spider grows as big as a dinner plate.

# Spiders Make Fascinating Pets

**12**

Some people share their homes with unusual exotic pets, such as spiders. These creatures are fun to watch. However, spiders are not hands-on pets. Like fish in an aquarium, they should be observed rather than handled.

There are many advantages to keeping a spider as a pet. Most can be purchased at a reasonable cost. They do not need to be fed every day. Their diet of crickets and other insects is easy to obtain. They do not require large or fancy housing. Their habitat needs to be cleaned just once per year. They are quiet and will not disturb the neighbors.

Chilean rose spiders are a good choice for a household pet.

A Chilean rose spider shedding its skin

Pet spiders do have a few disadvantages. They are escape artists. They can squeeze through tiny cracks. Spiders are fragile and easily injured. They may bite if stressed.

Tarantulas are popular pets. Some pet stores sell these large, hairy spiders. They can be kept in a small tank or terrarium. The bottom should be covered with peat moss or potting soil. A hollow log provides a hiding spot. A shallow dish of water and live crickets once or twice a week will keep the spider healthy.

## 800
**Approximate number of tarantula species found around the world.**

- Some people keep spiders as pets to observe.
- Spiders are inexpensive and easy to take care of.
- Spiders are easily injured if dropped and should not be handled.
- One of the most popular species of pet spider is the tarantula.

## SEEING DOUBLE

Tarantulas shed their exoskeletons. Before they molt, they lie on their backs with their legs spread. After molting, they leave behind a shell that looks like an exact replica of their bodies, without their heads and fangs.

# Fact Sheet

- Scientists have identified more than 43,000 spider species, but they believe there are many more.

- Spiders are found on all continents except Antarctica. Their habitat ranges from dry deserts to rain forests.

- Jumping spiders can jump 40 times their body length. Unlike many other spider species, they have sharp vision.

- Daddy longlegs are not members of the spider family. They have eight legs, but their pill-shaped bodies have only one section. They are more closely related to scorpions.

- Strong spider silk has many uses. It the past, it was woven into fishing nets and nylon stockings. It was even used as the crosshairs in guns to help precisely aim at targets.

- Spiderlings travel to different locations using a method called "ballooning." They release a strand of silken thread into the wind. Then, they float off to a new home.

- Many female spiders are at least twice the size of males. Bigger, heavier females lay more eggs. Smaller, lighter males can move around more rapidly to take advantage of more mating opportunities.

- The tarantella is a lively Italian folk dance between two partners. Legend says the name of the dance comes from two dancers who were the victims of a spider bite. They needed to move about frantically in order to be cured.

# Glossary

**amber**
A hard yellow fossil resin from trees.

**antihistamines**
Types of medicine used to treat reactions to substances, such as spider venom.

**arachnids**
A class of arthropods, including spiders, that have a body divided into two segments and eight legs.

**arachnophobia**
The fear of spiders.

**camouflage**
A protective coloration in animals that helps them blend in with their environments.

**exoskeleton**
The hard structure on the outside of a spider that supports and protects its insides.

**predators**
Animals that live by hunting, killing, and eating other animals.

**prey**
An animal that is hunted by other animals for food.

**spiderlings**
Young spiders.

**spinnerets**
Organs spiders use to produce silk.

**venom**
A poison produced by an animal and passed on to a victim.

# For More Information

## Books

Bishop, Nic. *Spiders*. New York: Scholastic Paperbacks, 2012.

Heos, Bridget. *Stronger than Steel: Spider Silk DNA and the Quest for Better Bulletproof Vests, Sutures, and Parachute Rope*. Boston: Houghton Mifflin Harcourt, 2013.

Marsh, Laura F. *Spiders*. Washington, DC: National Geographic, 2011.

## Visit 12StoryLibrary.com

Scan the code or use your school's login at **12StoryLibrary.com** for recent updates about this topic and a full digital version of this book. Enjoy free access to:

- Digital ebook
- Breaking news updates
- Live content feeds
- Videos, interactive maps, and graphics
- Additional web resources

**Note to educators:** Visit 12StoryLibrary.com/register to sign up for free premium website access. Enjoy live content plus a full digital version of every 12-Story Library book you own for every student at your school.

# Index

arachnid, 4–5

black widow, 7, 10–11, 20
brown recluse spider, 11
bubbles, 22–23

Cambodia, 19
claws, 4
crab spiders, 20–21, 25

diving bell spiders, 22–23

eggs, 5, 7–9
eyes, 4–5, 1–15, 18

fangs, 4–5, 7, 10, 18, 24, 27
fish-eating spiders, 19
fishing spiders, 22–23

funnel-web spiders, 12

goliath bird-eating spiders, 18–19, 24–25

Hawaiian happy-face spiders, 20–21

insects, 4, 12–13, 15–18, 22–23, 26

legs, 4–7, 9, 14–15, 18–19, 22, 24–25, 27

orb-weaver spiders, 14, 18

peacock spiders, 6–7, 20

pets, 26–27
predator, 4, 8–9, 18, 20–21
prey, 4–5, 12–15, 18–19, 21, 23, 25

silk, 5, 8–9, 12–13, 15, 17, 21–22
spiderlings, 8–9
spinnerets, 5, 8, 12–13

tarantulas, 10, 18–19, 24–25, 27
trapdoor spiders, 14–15

venom, 10, 17

webs, 5, 7–8, 12–15, 17–23, 25
wolf spiders, 8–9, 14–15, 19

## About the Author

Nancy Furstinger is the author of more than 100 books. She has been a feature writer for a daily newspaper, a managing editor of trade and consumer magazines, and an editor at children's book publishing houses. She lives in upstate New York with a menagerie of animals.

## READ MORE FROM 12-STORY LIBRARY

Every 12-Story Library book is available in many formats. For more information, visit 12StoryLibrary.com.